Footnotes

a book of digital art and poetry
Poetry and Modeling by Susan Cue

© Susan Cue, LLC 2024

Table of Contents

Dedication	5
Acknowledgements	7
The Grass Is Greener	8
January	10
Intertwine	13
Long Night	14
Lingering Feelings	17
Unnecessary Remarks	18
Sleepwalker	21
Storm Is Coming	22
Blue Sky	25
Purple Winter	27
Rain Dancing	29
Bella Falls	30
Hard Time	33
The Moon	34
Long Ride Home	37
The Color is Blue	38
The Hinoki Way	41
From the heart	42
About The Artist	45
Tips Before Bed	46
Epilogue	48

Feet tracks - Savannah
"The Journey Begins"

This progression takes the reader from optimism through intimacy, conflict, introspection, and environmental awareness, leading to a resolution that involves loss, growth, and eventual peace.

The Grass Is Greener: Self-discovery and optimism.
January: Time's passage and fleeting connections.
Intertwine: Intimacy's complexities prelude.
Long Night: Transition from intimacy to separation's chill.
Lingering Feeling: Endurance of relationship echoes.
Unnecessary Remarks: Conflict and truth's shadows.
Sleepwalker: Self-deception's consequences.
Storm Is Coming: Internal struggle, change's foreboding.
Blue Sky: Post-turmoil reflection, existential link.
Rain Dancing: Environmental consciousness, broader impact.
Bella Falls: Loss, regret, missed chances.
Hard Time: Growth's struggles, seeking clarity.
The Moon: Solitude's peace, natural cycles.
Long Ride Home: Healing journey, self-acceptance.
The Color is Blue: Transformation, overcoming betrayal.
The Hinoki Way - Peace and Joy.

"Book: How to Stop Worrying and Start Living by Dale Carnegie"

Dedication

To the transformative power of art, which has infused my life with inspiration and hope, reshaping my existence into a journey of peace and joy. In sharing my vision, I find a harmonious balance that aligns with the rhythm of my being. Poetry, my sanctuary, offered solace amidst the tumultuous waves and relentless flux of life. Photography, my lens to the world, allowed me to traverse the extraordinary landscapes of existence with a unique perspective. To the esteemed Guardian angels, dedicated social services providers, compassionate counselors, mentors, and foster parents who nurtured and believed in me during my formative years as a peculiar and misunderstood child and teenager.

Tio Randy and Mom Sandii - Love me without restrictions, My sister Yezenia for helping emancipate me from the group home hell.

Eagle Foot

Acknowledgments

This book wouldn't have been possible without the following:

Susan Cue - Poet, Model, Art Producer
Daniel Pineda - Digital Art Producer
Craig Lund - Editor / Layout Design
Ally Elliott - Editor
Jessica Ward - Landscape Photography
Evelin Ramirez - Photographer

The Grass Is Greener

Grab a chair, this will only take a minute
The grass is green, look around
Reach your hand out, grab it
It's yours
The man next to you has a testimony
I was lost, so eager, so stubborn
Closed to opinion, set in my own ways
Ran out of patience
Confusion sets in
The struggle of self deception
Ignorance and self doubt
Gives a sense of not belonging
Or knowing your calling
With this comes self empowerment.
A mission, a conquest
To what's rightfully yours.
The man sits quietly, at peace.

Book: "No excuses by Brian Tracy"

"Book: The Power of Concentration by Theron Q. Dumont"

January

Winter came with all its chills and the end of the year had no thrills.
Another routine day.
Grab two Grey Goose, take your shots, walk down the blvd to gather your thoughts.
The calming, warming in my gut
I breathe in the memories of yesterday. Wanting more.
Is this it I think?
Chance encounter with you brought back hope
You took me home, we listened to some
Jazzy tones.
With winter watching me nervously investigate the depths of passion letting out that dormant fire.
Satisfied, He walks me down the blvd.
We say goodbye with promises of tomorrow, yet tomorrow never comes.
Memories of that winter day stay alive in me.

"Alaska"

"Protect your mental space by remembering your worth and value."

"Intertwine"

Intertwine

Intertwine on this wine
with this fine line coming from my private Casanova
Lay me down on your dancing fingers
Unlace and embrace me
Kiss me down - all around
Even in your eyes, you can't deny
Roll the dice, is that ice?
Let me show you the ways I can shine
In the dark, maybe dawn
The reflection coming in
The reflection of us making music.

Long Night

Last Night seemed so long
My mate abandoned our love
Even though I resisted,
I let you know just how much I loved you
Last night seemed so long
Flashes of summer days and winter nights together Your kisses felt like harmony
Our lips locked and our bodies danced
I even looked over to see your figure
So masculine, so mighty
Lying next to me,
Accompanying me,
Playing with me,
All these things ran through my mind all night
Maybe ten thousand times,
Ten thousand rhymes
I gave you in that short moment
You were mine.

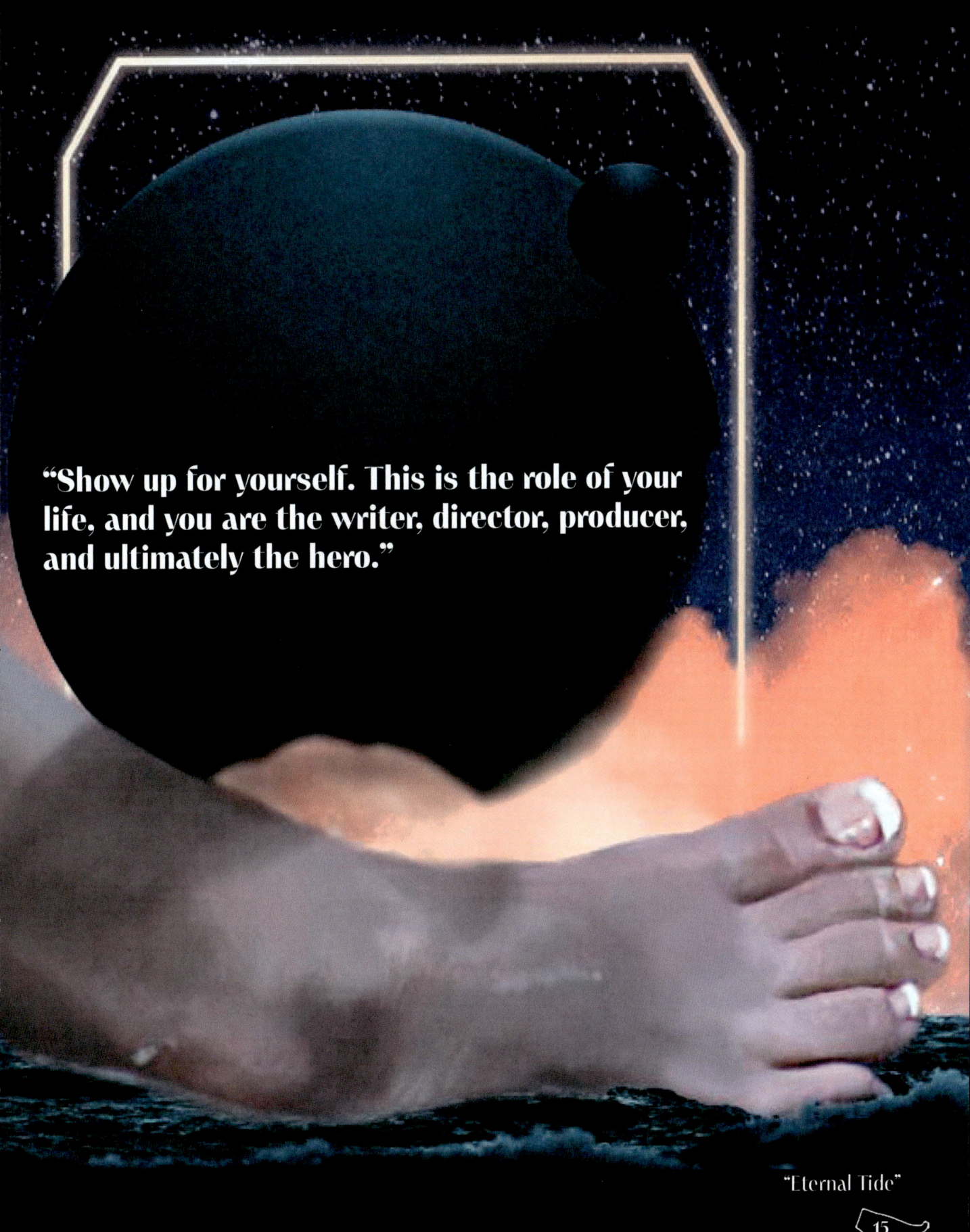

"Show up for yourself. This is the role of your life, and you are the writer, director, producer, and ultimately the hero."

"Eternal Tide"

Lingering Feelings

Just the other day I had that feeling,
You know that feeling, when two become one,
Not just for fun.
Let's widen our horizons, and look for the roses.
Do you smell them?
The gentle stroke of your cheek,
As we move in and smell the timeless goodbyes.
As the days go by, you give me that lingering feeling.

Unnecessary Remarks

Unnecessary remarks spew out like venomous bullshit.
The regret one gets just won't go unspoken.
Lies about how you really feel towards that sig-nificant other.
He leads you through the fields of emptiness.
So please tell me how you really feel.
Spare you and me.
That time will be short-lived because of the lies.

"Become like a compass, navigate and orient yourself to find a clear direction"

Sleepwalker

Open your eyes, it's time.
Wake up, Sleepwalker, wake up.
You walk through life so blindly.
You act so kindly,
Disguised in the skin of a politician.
So controversial yet contagious.
All eyes on you,
Such followers believing a man that's sleepwalking. Wake up, Sleepwalker, it's time.
Open your eyes, don't be blinded by the light.
Pull back the shame,
The shame that you seem to blame on Jane,
When she did nothing but comfort
All your pain.
Still, you thought she was very plain,
Because you had nothing to gain.
An easy conquest
Makes you shine.
One more soul to feed on,
Taking a new identity
And having nothing of your own.
How does it feel to walk through life so blind?

Storm is Coming

From a distance, wind blows at dawn. Moving the air so fast past the daily struggle. Be pretty, be happy. All you want is to blow like the wind. Move like a storm. Scream!

Please accept me with my pain and the storm I have in store.

It keeps moving, holding no prisoners.

Let go and move like the storm.

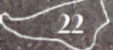

"Whispering Winds"

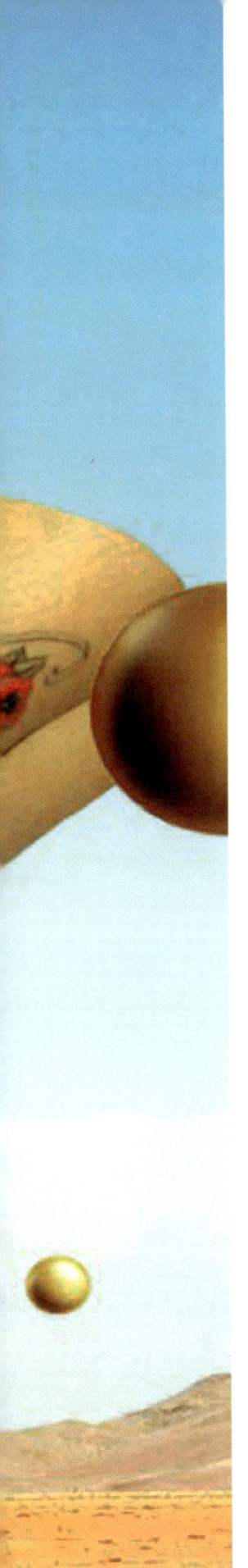

"Take a quiet moment to make a promise to yourself. First, declare your intention, then take action."

Blue Sky

The Blue sky stretching above the rolling green hills,
Over the sunset under the bridge, OMG!
Grappling with my fears..three AM now.
Over the moon a celestial whispers, my love for something.
My cheeks feel the cooling of my tears.
I will endure your pain.
Bring the Syringes, make you squeeze.
At ease.
It's a tango of release.
Today I woke up after a dream and now I'm in an institution.
I'm insane not to romance with this plan.
Let's go visit.

"Purple Winter"

Book: "The Stages of Life by Carl Jung"

Now and in this second, in these moments, amidst this thought;
Stop the noise. We are alive.
The call is eloquently powerful, resonating through deep silence.
We are free and alive. Just be.
Let's not vacuum the empty, anticipate nothing.
Silence surrounds us. Breathe in (Say in) and breathe out (Say Out).
Now, pause, Space will call you.
What do you want?
Think: I am Present.
No one will take that away.

"Enjoy the process of learning, Let go of the unknown and let your imagination create."

"Feet Fruit"

"Book: Awakened Imagination by Nevile Goddard"

Rain Dancing

Rain dances outside my window
Clearing the filth and pollution
"Oh mother nature how good you are"
Gasoline for my expensive car, fancy dancing shoes
More and more we seem to neglect you
Last nights festival "Oh what fun"
Only to find confetti, bottles, garbage all about
I wake to
No Earth. No Mother
I lay back to sleep and dream about the dancing rain.

Bella Falls

I took a trip to see you.

Didn't know it was the last time we would share life experience, laughter, love and pain.

I should have taken that last flight to see you.

I left you in San Francisco.

You called for me to come.

You declared your love, you asked me never to leave you.

I ran so fast! Past the memories at the Bungalow Suites, past the Comedy Club, made a left-turn,

another turn past the Presidential Suit.

I took a break to catch my breath of regret.

So I ran back It was too late a phone call told me you were gone .

Lost so much time. All regrets.

I will take it with pride.

"Bella Falls"

"Accept yourself to overcome the fear of judgement"

Hard Time

You gave me a hard time and I liked it.
Hot and cold.
We strolled through the rose garden, I pricked myself with a thorn.
Leading me now through rocky terrain. Like a rock climber, I need oxygen.
The high altitude has me seeing things.
I thought your hard time would let up. Like the weather, you're so unpredictable.
I need clarity to get back down.
This took my breath, afraid to climb, my life depended on it.
I descend into the abyss of space, never again to have your hard time.

The Moon

The moon illuminates my room;
 it moves through the room walking about
shining it's bright light
on my face
I put the shades down and still you
peep through not to be ignored.
Lonely, longing for some company;
I feel the moon's peace and stillness.
I take it in and become the same.
We fall deep asleep into the realm of
space and time.
Not to be ignored.

"Book: The Laws of Human Nature by Robert Green"

Long Ride Home

Lost my soul, lost my mind, lost myself
A long ride back, the road looks dark with no hope in sight,
no direction, the flashing lights pass me by
I don't want to stop, I just want to ride the long way back
Lost my voice, lost my smile, lost and alone
Looks like I am almost home
The fresh air as the fog moves out fills my lungs as
I now choose life and inhale
Almost home the sun rises bright in my eyes and
it wakes me from my broken self.
I am home, I am safe, I am free.
I exhale.

The Color is Blue

Blue necklace, reckless words,
you put it on me.
It's a gift, the big reveal,
not for me, another lover.
BLUE is what you made me feel.
I so wanted to believe you.
I didn't want to rip the bandage off.
I was not ready to heal.
I was not ready to deal with letting go.
Had blinders.
I wanted you to come home and
make everything better.
I hate the color blue.
I don't want to be a new shade of blue.

"Book: The power of Subconscious Mind by Joseph Murphy(1963)"

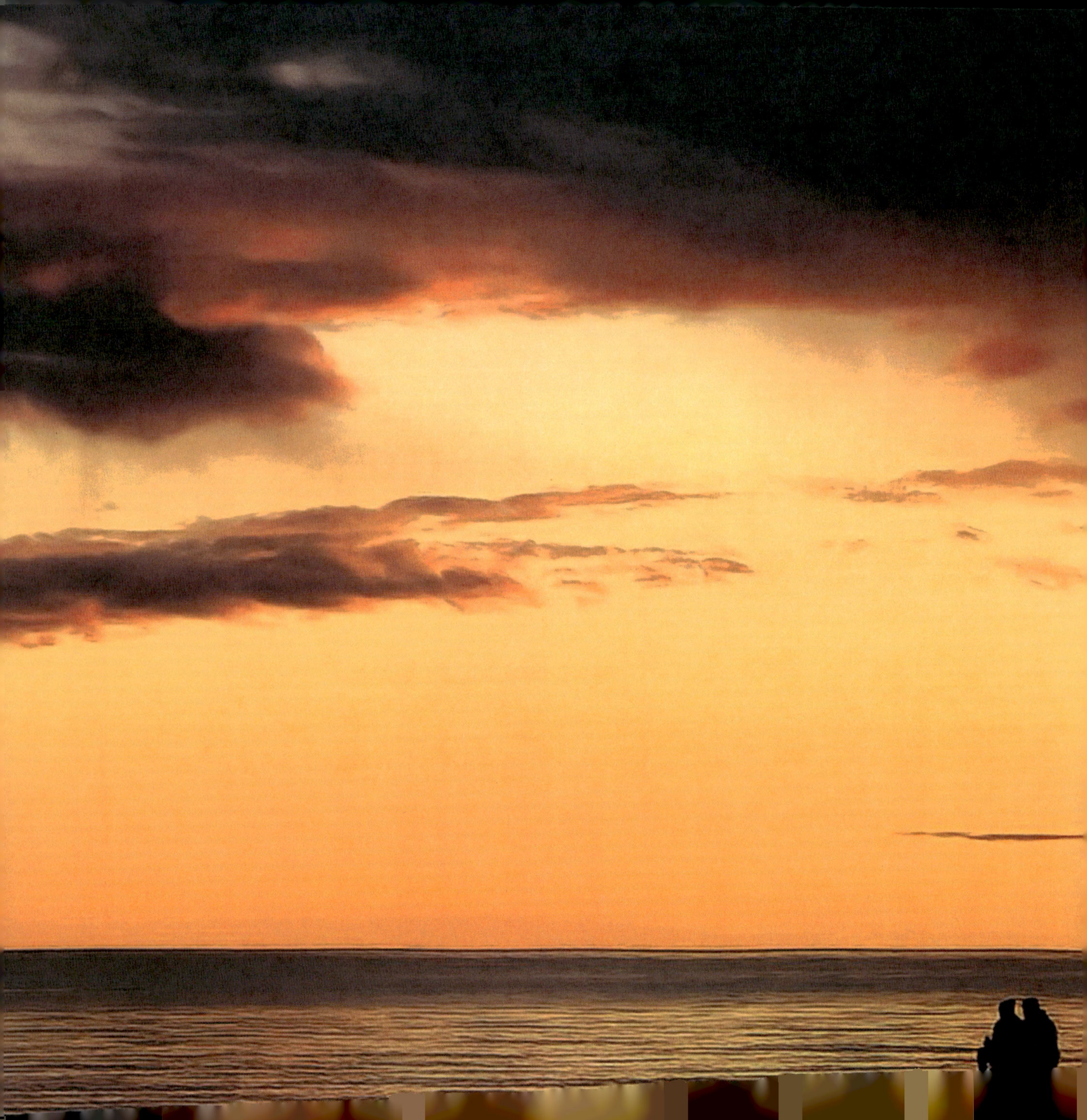

Hanok K-Beauty - Los Angeles, CA

The Hinoki Way

Sounds weave through existence, a symphony of moments of life, birds sing their tales. Tides rise and fall, whispering impermanence. Transcending the deepest feeling, like distant thunder—a constant reminder. Amidst it all, find space to grow, to become. We are lonely together, yet not alone

Facts

"In Japan, the Hinoki Cypress is a significant timber tree utilized in both art and construction. An ancient Japanese text praised the Hinoki Cypress as 'an excellent tree for building structures.' This tree symbolizes the harmonious relationship between nature and humanity, respecting the natural order."

From the Heart

- Clean out your clutter: Give away items like clothing, books, pots, tools, and toys to friends who might need them.
- Offer to run errands: Help someone by running errands for them or giving them a ride.
- Organize a clean-up party: Gather friends to clean up a park, neighborhood, or beach.
- Babysit for free: Offer free babysitting services to friends or relatives.
- Volunteer: Spend time helping out at a local shelter.
- Write a letter: Send a letter or email to someone who has made a difference in your life.
- Make hygiene bags: Create bags with essential items and drop them off at a shelter.
- Bake goodies: Bake treats and share them with your coworkers or neighbors.
- Donate to animal shelters: Purchase dog and cat food or blankets.

Quotes

"Life will present you with people and circumstances to reveal when you're not free."
— Peter Crone

"What stands in the way becomes the way."
— School of Greatness, Lewis Howes

"The more you shine, the more shadows you cast."
— Shi Heng Yi

"Defeat is a state of mind; no one is ever defeated until defeat has been accepted as a reality."
— Bruce Lee

"Silence - Radio Station - non-stop thinking"

"Hinoki cannot be fully appreciated until it has been observed inside out, and through all four seasons."
— Myeongjae's descendant of the 13th generation, WanSik YOON

"Forgive yourself for not knowing what you didn't know before you learned it."
— Maya Angelou

"No one gets away with anything, ever. Take responsibility for your own life."
— Jordan Peterson

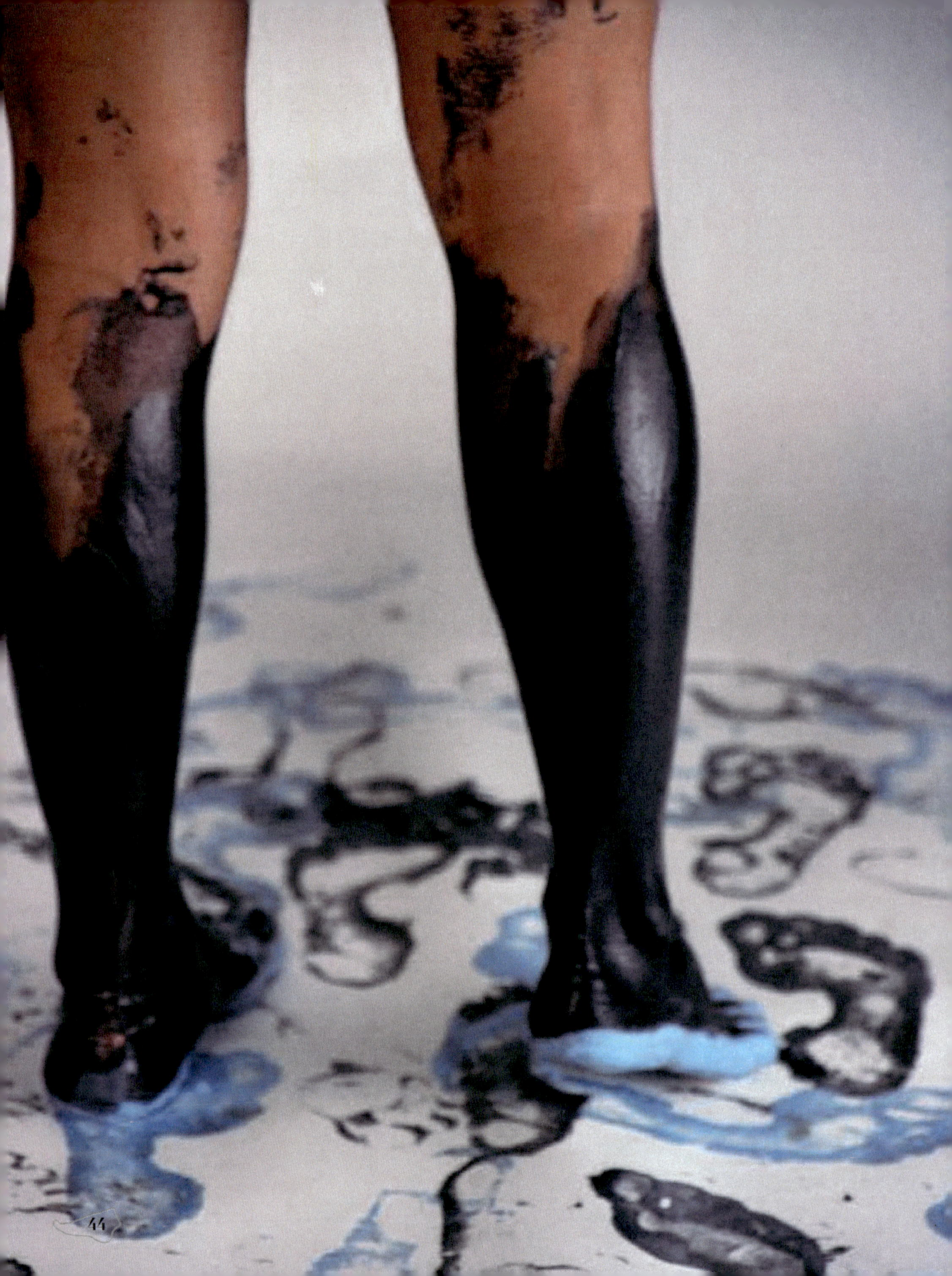

About the Artist

Born in Mexico and moving to Los Angeles at the tender age of four, my life took a turn that led me into foster care due to my family's financial struggles. The journey was tough, with my sisters and I eventually finding a home with our aunt and uncle in the Bay Area. They were my bridge to a new language and a new beginning, even sending me to an all-girls Catholic boarding school in Spokane, Washington.

However, that setting wasn't the right fit for me, and after navigating through various foster homes, I found myself at a crossroads in a closing group home. Facing the prospect of juvenile detention for lack of other options, I chose a different path and petitioned the court for emancipation.

With a job and community college on my resume, I earned my freedom. That freedom led me to a film school, where I dove into workshops and explored different departments, sparking my own creative fire. My education continued at Santa Monica College, where I studied Business and Broadcasting.

This journey culminated in a significant achievement: producing and hosting a segment at the AFI Lifetime Achievement Award for Al Pacino. My story is one of finding strength and authority within myself through expression, education, and creativity. It's about the importance of growth and spirituality for a balanced life.

And it's a reminder to always **'Pay It Forward,'** sharing the lessons learned with others on their paths. Contact me at info@susancue.com

Tips Before Bed: Relaxing Nighttime Foot Soak

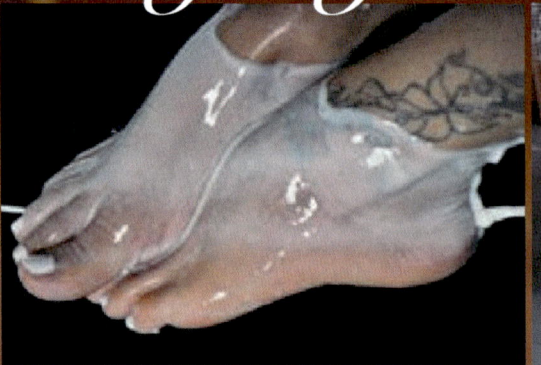

Prep Your Soothing Soak:
Begin your nighttime ritual by filling a basin with warm, inviting water. Add a generous scoop of Epsom salts and a few drops of your favorite essential oils or bath oil to create a fragrant, relaxing experience. Submerge your feet and let them bask in the warmth for a few minutes. Feel the gentle tingling sensation as your feet begin to relax – it's truly a delightful treat.

Homemade Massage Scrub Ingredients:
1/2 cup sea salt
1/2 a fresh lemon
1-2 teaspoons of olive oil

Craft Your Scrub and Massage Away:
Combine the sea salt, fresh lemon juice, and olive oil in a bowl. Stir until you have a cohesive mixture.

Sit back comfortably and apply the scrub to your feet. Start with your thumb on top and fingers cradling the arch. Gently massage the mixture into your skin, focusing on the soles and working your way from the ankles down to the toes.

Apply firm pressure along the arches and sides of your feet with your thumbs and fingers. This helps in releasing the day's tensions. Use circular motions with your thumbs, moving from the back of the heel to the base of each foot. This technique aids in soothing deep foot muscles. Finish by gently wiggling your toes and giving your hands a good shake to release any accumulated stress.

This pre-bedtime ritual not only soothes tired feet but also prepares your mind and body for a restful night's sleep. Enjoy the serene journey from the day's hustle to peaceful slumber.

47

Epilogue

"The Victorious Attitude: A Classical Guide to Success" by Marden encourages you to embrace your inner strength. Remember, it's okay to prioritize yourself. Feel deeply, breathe silently, and release. Let your tears flow—they cleanse and pave the way for renewal. Put your intentions into action, for every moment holds the potential for transformation.

"Accept failure on your road to success. Find mistakes in logic"

Made in the USA
Las Vegas, NV
17 April 2025